Feeling Happy

by Helen Frost

Consulting Editor: Gail Saunders-Smith, Ph.D.

Consultant: Erik Willcutt, Ph.D.
Child Clinical Psychologist
Instructor, University of Denver

Pebble Books

an imprint of Capstone Press
Mankato, Minnesota

Pebble Books are published by Capstone Press
1710 Roe Crest Drive, North Mankato, Minnesota 56003
www.capstonepress.com

102012
006929R
Library of Congress Cataloging-in-Publication Data
Frost, Helen, 1949–
    Feeling happy / by Helen Frost.
    p. cm.—(Emotions)
    Includes bibliographical references and index.
    Summary: Simple text and photographs describe and illustrate happiness and
how to enjoy it.
    ISBN-13: 978-0-7368-0669-5 (hardcover)
    ISBN-10: 0-7368-0669-5 (hardcover)
    ISBN-13: 978-0-7368-4844-2 (softcover pbk.)
    ISBN-10: 0-7368-4844-4 (softcover pbk.)
    1. Happiness in children—Juvenile literature. [1. Happiness.] I. Title.
II. Emotions. (Mankato, Minn.)
BF723.H37F76 2001
152.4′2—dc21   00-025020

Note to Parents and Teachers

The Emotions series supports national health education standards related to interpersonal communication and expression of feelings. This book describes and illustrates the feeling of happiness. The photographs support emergent readers in understanding the text. The repetition of words and phrases helps emergent readers learn new words. This book also introduces emergent readers to subject-specific vocabulary words, which are defined in the Words to Know section. Emergent readers may need assistance to read some words and to use the Table of Contents, Words to Know, Read More, Internet Sites, and Index/Word List sections of the book.

Table of Contents

You feel good
when you are happy.

You feel cheerful
when you are happy.

You smile when
you are happy.

You might laugh
when you are happy.

You might sing
when you are happy.

Reading books might
make you happy.

Playing sports might make you happy.

Helping people might make you happy.

You can share
your happiness.

cheerful—happy and lively

happiness—a feeling of being pleased and contented

laugh—to make a sound that shows you think that something is funny

smile—to widen your mouth and turn it up at the corners to show you are happy; a smile is one way to share happiness with other people.

Read More

Crary, Elizabeth and Shari Steelsmith. *When You're Happy and You Know It: Feelings for Little Children.* Seattle: Parenting Press, 1996.

Doudna, Kelly. *I Feel Happy.* How Do You Feel? Minneapolis: Abdo Publishing, 1999.

Leonard, Marcia. *Happy.* How I Feel. Bethany, Mo.: Fitzgerald Books, 1998.

Parr, Todd. *Things That Make You Feel Good/Things That Make You Feel Bad.* Boston: Little, Brown and Company, 1999.

Internet Sites

FactHound offers a safe, fun way to find Internet sites related to this book. All of the sites on FactHound have been researched by our staff.

Here's all you do:

Visit *www.facthound.com*

FactHound will fetch the best sites for you!   23

Index/Word List

books, 15
cheerful, 7
feel, 5, 7
good, 5
happiness, 21
helping, 19
laugh, 11

people, 19
playing, 17
reading, 15
share, 21
sing, 13
smile, 9
sports, 17

Word Count: 57
Early-Intervention Level: 6

Editorial Credits
Mari C. Schuh, editor; Kia Bielke, designer; Katy Kudela, photo researcher

Photo Credits
Anthony Nex/Pictor, 4
Index Stock Imagery, 12
Marilyn Moseley LaMantia, 10
PhotoDisc, Inc., 1, 14
Photo Network/Cynthia Salter, 6; Photo Network/Aristock/Bill Lai, 8
Pictor, cover, 18
Unicorn Stock Photos/Aneal Vohra, 16; Joel Dexter, 20

The author thanks the children's section staff at the Allen County Public Library in Fort Wayne, Indiana, for research assistance.